Plug-Parent's Life's Ultimate Gifts

"Steps to Raising Healthy Children in a World of Insanity"

Parents Life's Ultimate Gift LLC

Copyright Page
Plug-Parents Life's Ultimate Gift
"Steps to Raising Healthy Children
In A World of Insanity"

Copyright © 2024
Published by Delores A. Wallace
Miami Florida
Paperback ISBN: 979-8-89504-357-8
Printed in Dade County
First Edition 2024

Interior design by Arilia Winn

Library of Congress Cataloging -in-Publication Data

PLUG - Parents Life's Ultimate Gift
"Steps To Raising Healthy Children in A World of Insanity"

Table of Contents

Acknowledgements

Creating this book has been an incredible journey, and I am immensely grateful to all those who have supported me along the way.

A very special thank you to my editor, Taaj Williams. Your exceptional insights, meticulous attention to detail, and unwavering commitment to excellence have been invaluable to this project. Your dedication and hard work have significantly enhanced the quality of this book, and for that, I am deeply thankful.

Taaj, your guidance and expertise have not only improved this manuscript but have also made me a better writer. Your patience and encouragement throughout this process have been a source of inspiration and motivation. I am truly fortunate to have had the opportunity to work with someone as talented and passionate as you.

With sincere gratitude,
Delores A. Wallace
The Parent Plug

Foreword

This book aims to assist parents and educators in understanding the importance of collaboration for the future well-being of our children. Regardless of whether you're raising a child in pre-K or guiding a college student, the challenges we face today have become increasingly tangible due to the everyday pressures confronting both our children and educators. You might wonder what sets "Plug-Parent's Life's Ultimate Gifts" apart from other handbooks. The answer lies in you and the significant issues our children encounter in securing a safe environment within their schools. Crafting this parent handbook required considerable effort to ensure it serves as a valuable informational resource for parents, guardians, and caregivers.

I'd like to elaborate on why I chose to embark on this endeavor and create something parents can turn to amidst the complexities of education. With over 35 years of experience in various educational settings, I vividly recall my early days in the field and a simple question posed by my then-boss: "If every parent withdraws their child, where will we be?" My response: Unemployed. This question fueled my work with compassion, despite being undervalued and underpaid in the educational hierarchy and industry. I firmly believed my role was paramount in ensuring parents were integral to their children's education. Serving as a Community Outreach Coordinator and Parent Coordinator, I approached my responsibilities with utmost seriousness, recognizing the stakes for our children.

How does one navigate their child's education in a world fraught with challenges? Many of you have already mastered this delicate balancing act, striving to shield and encourage your children from external influences. In academia, there's been a noticeable shift in perspectives over the past two decades. The title of this handbook prompts you to ponder, "How can we, as a society, continue to raise our children in a World of Insanity?" This question resonates with parents entrusting their children to schools, fervently praying for their guidance and safety. Sadly, school violence persists because genuine issues remain unaddressed, jeopardizing our children's safety and educational pursuits.

Education stands as one of society's most invaluable tools. How can we impress upon our children's schools the importance of fostering a safe and nurturing environment? How can we contribute to a world where children feel compelled to march in protest, demanding their right to a secure education? Such circumstances shouldn't prevail, and together, we can safeguard our children and ensure they receive a quality education.

This handbook underscores the power of parents as the most potent force: "Plug: Parent's Life's Ultimate Gift." Drawing from my extensive experience in education, particularly in a role often perceived as insignificant, I emphasize the pivotal role of parents. As a District Parent Coordinator, I had the privilege of collaborating with exceptional parents in our communities, fueling my passion despite external perceptions of my role's significance. If parents were to withdraw their children from schools, the necessity for positions such as Superintendents, Principals, and Teachers would be obsolete. My conviction always remained: I worked for you, the parent. This handbook aims to support you as you navigate through the ever-evolving challenges within the educational system.

I extend my heartfelt gratitude to every parent in Essex County with whom I've had the privilege of assisting on their children's educational journey. To every teacher, principal, and colleague, serving as your Community Outreach Coordinator and Parent Coordinator has been immensely fulfilling, even during the most challenging times.

Preface

I dedicate this book to my late sister, Barbara Joyce Wallace, and my late brother, Keith Allen Wallace, who selflessly served our communities. Heartfelt thanks are extended to my sons, Nicklaus and Jeremy Wallace, for their unwavering support as their mother advocated for numerous families over the past three decades. I am grateful to my sister, Alizina Wallace McCoy, whose encouragement reinforced the significance of my work for parents and students. I am thankful for all the families I've had the privilege of working with over the years, guiding them toward success. Furthermore, I appreciate the Superintendents, Principals, Teachers, Guidance Counselors, bus drivers, and custodians who embraced my dedication to caring for families within the district.

I express my gratitude to our Heavenly Father for instilling in me a genuine concern for our children's education and for illuminating the pivotal role parents play in this equation.

Admittedly, I had apprehensions about writing this book. I came to understand that fear can hinder us, making us believe we have nothing to offer. This journey has been profound, and it has been a privilege to serve my community. My previous roles have ignited in me a desire to do more and give more. Why not begin here? I am committed to continuing to help families realize they are the PLUG - Parent's Life's Ultimate Gift. In acknowledging the divine presence in our lives, I recognize that without God, there would be no "Us," and without "Us," there would be no "Them" (our children).

The basis of this handbook is presented in 7 parts throughout 6 chapters:

1. What does Parental Involvement look like Post-COVID-19?
2. Where is Parental Involvement after the Covid-19 Pandemic?
3. Why is Parental Involvement necessary for children's Success in Pre-K-College?
4. How to Increase Parental Involvement in a World of Insanity?
5. School/Community Engagement
6. Running an Effective Parent Group
7. Social Media/Cyber Bullying

Now, let's dive in.

Chapter One: The Changing Landscape of the Education System and Parental Involvement

As I reflect on my years in education across various levels, I've witnessed the subtle yet significant changes unfolding within the educational system. While some shifts were unnoticeable to many, a strong sense of transformation was spreaded throughout the atmosphere. It became evident that societal dynamics were evolving, influencing individuals' perspectives and priorities. On some days within my office and shared spaces, I observed different discussions with viewpoints emerging regarding the direction of our educational system. Some remained steadfast in their commitment to delivering the best education for children, while others seemed preoccupied with titles and monetary gains. Furthermore, in 2004 I began to notice that some new teachers coming out of college would only stay two to three years in our district, if that long and with no vested interest in our children and communities. Ambition and aspirations to advance professionally are commendable, yet true leadership entails a willingness to roll up one's sleeves and serve.

1. What does Parental Involvement look like post-COVID-19?

The onset of the COVID-19 pandemic and the surge in gun violence have reshaped parental involvement, necessitating a shift towards digital communication. Platforms like Zoom have facilitated monthly parent meetings, enabling parents to voice concerns about challenges facing our children today. The convenience of social media and mobile apps has made it easier for parents to stay abreast of classroom updates and changes, review assignments, and monitor grades. However, the adoption of technology hinges on parents' comfort and willingness to engage with these tools.

2. Where is Parental Involvement after the Covid-19 Pandemic?

Parental involvement has increased in the wake of the pandemic, offering parents a more flexible approach to participating in PTA meetings without leaving their homes. The Department of Education's website and school portals provide information on parental involvement policies, underscoring the importance of parental engagement in children's educational journey. See "Parental Involvement Title 1 Part A."[1]

The evolving educational landscape demands heightened parental involvement, considering the challenges confronting teachers and students alike.

---

1   Parental Involvement Title 1 Part A, please click on this link: https://www2.ed.gov/programs/titleiparta/parentinvguid.doc

The concept of "it takes a village" rings true in education, emphasizing the indispensable roles of schools, communities, and parents. Schools should regard parents as equal partners in decision-making processes affecting their children's education. Strengthening collaboration between parents, administrators, teachers, and student's post-pandemic is imperative to address disruptions in the educational process and foster a conducive learning environment.

Amidst the challenges posed by the pandemic, families have grappled with social-emotional hardships, reinforcing the need for parental voices in education. Parental involvement encompasses participation in PTA, PTSA, and PTO meetings, alongside engagement in School Board, grade level, safety, Child Study Team, and nutrition meetings. These forums are extremely important for parents to actively contribute to decisions shaping their children's educational experiences. With all the changes that are taking place in education, as a parent, you need to be in the room when these changes are being decided.

As an advocate for parental involvement, I've emphasized the significance of parents' presence during decision-making processes. Your voice matters, and your active participation in School Board meetings ensures transparency and accountability in educational reforms. The accessibility afforded by virtual platforms like Zoom enhances parental engagement, enabling parents to balance professional obligations while staying informed about educational developments.

As we navigate the post-COVID educational landscape, increased parental involvement promises a brighter future for our children, notwithstanding the challenges some families may encounter. Remember, your voice matters on multiple levels, shaping the educational trajectory of our collective future.

Remember this formula as you plan your schedules: Monthly PTA +1 ½ hours rather Zoom or in person = less than 12 hours per school year.

The image above illustrates a solid teacher-parent relationship to ensure the child's holistic development.

Chapter Two: Why Parents Are the Secret Sauce from Pre-K to College

Let's tackle this next question:

3. Why is Parental Involvement necessary for children's Success in Pre-K through College?

Why do parents need to stay in the game from Pre-K all the way through college? Some might think, "Hey, my job is done once my child hits college," and if that's you, Congratulations! You've done a fantastic job! I, on the other hand, strongly believe that parents are the Secret Sauce from Pre-K to the completion of college. We just have to switch our approach for college to support the young adult with learning effective communication skills and how to advocate for themselves.

Now, in the past 15 years, I've seen some shifts in our education system. Not that good things aren't happening, mind you, but sometimes it feels like it's more about who you know rather than what you know. We've got to prepare future leaders who truly understand the value of each and every child in shaping our tomorrow. Just look at the rise in gun violence and bullying – it's a crisis that's hitting home for parents and students everywhere, whether you're in the city or the suburbs. That's why parental involvement is crucial. We can do better if we all chip in a little more and become active participants in our childrens' education.

For those of you already proactively involved from Pre-K to college, you are ahead of the curve and headed in the right direction! You're setting the pace and laying the solid foundation, so keep up the good work! As I mentioned earlier, this need for parental involvement is more apparent now than ever, especially post-pandemic. Community and parental involvement are like the dynamic duo in the education world. Just think about it – the whole point of the education system is to help our children become their best. Always remember, without parents and children, there wouldn't be a need for Superintendents, Administrators, Teachers, Teachers' Aides, Guidance Counselors, Child Study Teams, or School Boards. They would not exist. Which is why being a parent who advocates for our children is so important – your voice is essential and it matters. Refer back to the formula mentioned in Chapter 1 for the time to allot for school meetings. For parents with more than one child in school at different locations, strongly consider taking terms with each school.

4. How to Increase Parental Involvement in a World of Insanity?

Increasing parental involvement can smooth out the bumps in your and your child's school journey as you get more acquainted with the school's environment. The superintendent plays a crucial role here, setting the tone for the entire district. They have the power to build a district up from the inside out, and this starts with building a solid foundation of school/community that embraces parental involvement. By emphasizing the importance of parental involvement right from the start, parents get a clear signal that they're valued partners in their child's education. Creating a campaign to promote parent organizations such as PTA or PTSA, should occur before the start of each new school year. The monthly meetings are likely to power-up your child's growth and development throughout the school year.

Making sure every parent knows who's who in the PTA, PTSA, and PTO should be a priority. They are like the unsung heroes, working behind the scenes to make magic happen in our schools. And every superintendent should ensure there's a District Parent Council in place, giving parents a direct line to the decision-making process. After all, parents are the MVPs in this game called education, and they deserve to be front and center when decisions impacting their children and their children's education are being made.

Now, let's talk about the real game-changer: technology. It's a tool we can't afford to ignore. Schools should be leveraging every tech trick in the book – from Robo Calls to text messaging, emails, and beyond – to keep parents in the loop. Transparent communication is key. Most schools have those handy message boards outside, giving parents and the community a sneak peek into what's happening daily. The more transparent, the better our kids' future looks.

Chapter Three: Supercharging Parental Involvement: A Superintendent's Playbook

Can we talk about how superintendents can help parents and students come out on top? Some of the most crucial information concerning your children's education and well-being is done in the meetings without parent representation. Here's a playbook of winning strategies:

1. Put PTA officers' names on display where everyone can see them – whether it's in the school lobby or on the website. This shows that the school has an active parent board.
2. Make sure the PTA calendar with all parent meetings is posted everywhere – from the school office to the website and even in local community spots like churches and other establishments that will permit this. Monthly reminders by way of school newsletters and text messaging are also helpful.
3. Connect your school's PTA with the State and National PTA. These organizations are essential for the growth of your PTA officers.
4. Ensure PTO receive training in their duties and responsibilities from State and National PTA members.
5. Keep the PTA's bank account separate from school accounts. Transparency is key.

6.   Encourage everyone – administrators, teachers, parents, local officials, Chamber of Commerce members, and students – to join the PTA.

7.   Show up and spread the word! Ask to join community events and set up a table with info about your school's PTA[2].

8.   Send 1-2 representatives to National PTA conferences. It's a game-changer for your PTA's growth.

9.   Budget for light refreshments or get local restaurants to donate for meetings held after work. Everyone loves snacks!

10.   End the school year on a high note with a celebration of success for everyone. You've earned it!

11.   Ensure your PTA board includes a school administrator, teacher, and community member to represent all stakeholders across the school-community network.

12.   Connect with other local PTA's in the district three times for networking opportunities to hold forums. This is an opportunity to know what is happening in other schools and help build a strong community connection. Collaboration is key.

13.   Encourage parent groups to gather according to grade-groups and share ideas.

14.   School Safety Committee parents should have a representative from the parent board or parent membership in these meetings. These meetings are usually during the day. If you cannot get a representative to attend during the day, the principal holds one meeting

---

2   Visit the PTA website for more information. www.pta.org/

with a parent representative via Zoom. This can be
done with a parent attending once or twice a year.
15.   Schedule meetings with local law enforcement or
the Mayor's Office to discuss school safety. This can
be done in-person or virtual. Safety first, always.

If your school or district already has a District Parent
Involvement Policy in place, pat yourselves on the back – you're
ahead of the game. Keep up the fantastic work, and remember,
when students, teachers, and parents come together, magic
happens!

The image above indicates collaboration between students, teachers, and parents to ensure everyone's objectives are met.

Chapter Four: Building Bridges Between School and Community

5. School/Community Engagement

We can bridge the gap between our schools and our communities and it's all about bringing everyone together to work and build strong relationships and support networks. Here's how we can make it happen:

1. **Community Forums**: Host forums that bring together parents, students, administrators, and community leaders. It's a fantastic way to increase awareness and support from all stakeholders.

2. **Engaging Community Leaders**: Get city officials, mayors, city councils, and local businesses involved. Their support can make a world of difference, whether it's through tutoring programs or providing social and emotional support for students and families.

3. **Boosting Student Achievement**: Let's make raising student achievement a community-wide campaign[3]. We want our kids to be excited about learning and achieving their best. And hey, why not have a parent on the school's curriculum committee? Parents are a crucial part of the school community, and they

---

3   https://www.ed.gov/news/press-releases/us-department-education-creates-national-parents-and-families-engagement-council-help-ensure-recovery-efforts-meet-students%E2%80%99-needs (US Department of Education/June 2022).

should have a say in decisions affecting their kids' education. I am not saying parents should run the schools. Parents should be full partners in some of the decisions concerning their children's education.

4. **Stay Informed**: Parents, make sure you stay updated and in the loop about local and state educational decisions. Sign up for the monthly Register from the Department of Education and stay plugged into what's happening in your child's school and beyond.

5. **Transparency is Key**: School districts that are transparent about educational policies, mental health, and school safety create an environment where students can thrive. Districts need to do more to ensure our kids are safe, and that starts with parents getting involved in local politics, getting to know the elected officials, and holding them accountable. For four basic types of evaluations that can be integrated into the existing structure of most schools, refer to Daniel J. Flannery's article - "Improving School Violence Prevention Programs through Meaningful Evaluation."[4]

6. Running an Effective Parent Group

In most cases, K-6 grade parents are motivated and excited to be involved in what is happening in their children's schools. Especially now, with the number of school cases of violence, parents are taking on more of an active role. Running an influential Parent Group requires support and a need to make parents feel they are essential to their children's educational progress. In today's world, our children face so many dilemmas. Parents are

---

4   https://eric.ed.gov/?id=ED417244

their children's Greatest Advocates. Parents groups have been around for decades, and the need today is much more significant due to the generational changes in how our society copes with school violence, among other issues.

What makes parental groups important?

1. Strong Leadership in Parents
2. Contact Local, State, and National PTA for training workshops for parents.
3. Becoming a member of your child's PTA
4. PTA School Elections
5. Set up a PTA Bank Account for all fundraising and PTA dues!
6. Marketing Strategies through social media
7. Promote School Spirit
8. Plan meetings where teachers can attend.
9. Promote college school fairs.
10. Promote career school fairs.
11. Become a Parent of Schools Nutrition Program
12. Make sure there is a District Parent Council through the Superintendent's Office.
13. Parents understand they are the Ultimate Gift to their children's education.
14. Taking more of an active role in schools' curriculum choices
15. Attending grade-level meetings.
16. Receiving electronic information from schools, community, state, and federal agencies

on educational policy and issues.
17.   Active parent forums with schools'
administrators and community members.
18.   Attend monthly parent Zoom meetings.
19.   Make your PTA meeting minutes
available online for parents!
20.   Take advantage of the Social Media
platforms to promote your schools' activities!
21.   Promote your PTA membership
drive in the School Newsletters
22.   Promote School Spirit by engaging in various
activities and events to help support the school.
23.   Always handle fundraising events in a manner that
allows the Treasurer to manage the accounts efficiently
according to the National PTA/PTO guidelines.
24.   Attend monthly meetings at
least 4 to 5 times a month.
25.   All meetings held for Parents, including
the ESL meetings, should be combined to
help parents get to know one another.
26.   Celebrate by including everyone to
become an advocate for all children.
27.   Grade-level parent meetings by supporting
the academics and athletic departments.
28.   Foster a Positive Learning Environment at
Home: Encourage and support your child's learning
by creating a dedicated study space, setting a routine,
and showing interest in their academic progress.

29.   Collaborate with Teachers and Staff: Build
strong relationships with your child's teachers
and school staff. Regular communication can
help address any concerns early and ensure your
child is receiving the support they need.

30.   Volunteer for School Activities and Events: Offer
your time and skills for various school functions, whether
it's chaperoning field trips, helping with school plays,
or organizing community events. Active participation
can enhance the school experience for all students.

Let's celebrate the power of parental involvement and continue working together to advocate for all children's education. Together, we can make a real difference!

Chapter Five: Navigating Social Media and Cyberbullying

As we discuss the world of social media and cyberbullying – two topics that have become hot-button issues in education as both are used as tools to help our students improve their overall experiences. Social media isn't just a fad anymore; it's an integral part of our lives, and it's here to stay. But like any powerful tool, it comes with its pros and cons. Let's break it down:

The Pros of Social Media:

1. **Connecting with Parents and Community**: Social media provides a platform for schools to connect with parents and the community, sharing information about academics, events, and important updates.

2. **Effective Communication**: With just a click of a button, schools can quickly disseminate information to parents and stakeholders instantly. Sending flyers for meetings is at your fingertips. This makes it easier for members of the PTA and the executive board to be more effective in timely communications.

3. **Enhanced Parental Involvement**: Social media has made it easier for parents to stay engaged in their children's education. Those in charge of communications can ensure parents are aware of meetings, workshops, board meetings, and school events.

The Cons of Social Media:

1.   **Insecurities and Pressure**: Social media has created an environment where people's insecurities are on display for the world to see. For younger generations especially, there's a constant pressure to fit in and measure up to unrealistic standards set by social media.

2.   **Cyberbullying**: Unfortunately, social media has also become a breeding ground for cyberbullying. It's all too easy for students to feel insecure and hide behind screens and torment their peers, causing lasting emotional harm.

So, what can schools do to navigate this digital landscape responsibly?

1.   **Education and Awareness**: Schools should educate students, parents, and staff about the risks of social media and cyberbullying. Awareness is the first step in prevention.

2.   **Promoting Positive Online Behavior**: Encourage students to use social media responsibly, promoting kindness and empathy in their interactions.

3.   **Establishing Clear Policies**: Schools should have clear policies in place to address cyberbullying and online harassment, with consequences for those who violate these policies.

4.   **Support Systems**: Provide support systems for students who are victims of cyberbullying, including counseling services and peer support groups.

5.   **Parental Involvement**: Parents should actively monitor their children's online activity and have open conversations about responsible social media use.

By working together as a community, we can harness the power of social media for good while mitigating the risks associated with its use. The more widely used, the more sophisticated in gathering data and information. Let's empower our students to be responsible digital citizens and create a safer online environment for all.

Chapter Six: Navigating Parental Engagement in the Age of COVID-19

The COVID-19 pandemic has reshaped the landscape of parental involvement in schools. With social distancing measures in place, PTAs and parents have had to adapt to new ways of communication and collaboration. Here are some strategies to navigate parental engagement during these challenging times:

1. **Utilize Technology**: Many PTAs have successfully transitioned to web and app-based platforms to maintain communication and engagement. Explore resources provided by your state PTA and National PTA for guidance on using technology effectively.

2. **Create Online Communities**: Consider establishing a school community blog where parents and teachers can discuss relevant topics and share ideas. This can help foster a sense of community and collaboration, even in a virtual setting.

3. **Parent Involvement in Hiring Process**: Advocate for parental representation in the hiring process for teachers, administrators, and superintendents. Having diverse perspectives at the table ensures fair and inclusive decision-making.

4. **Volunteer Opportunities**: Encourage parents to volunteer for various projects and initiatives within the school, even if their schedules are busy. Attending monthly meetings, keeping in touch with

teachers, and actively participating in school board meetings are essential ways to stay engaged.

5. **PTA Membership Campaigns**: Launch campaigns to promote PTA membership and highlight the benefits of joining. Emphasize the importance of parental involvement in supporting student success.

Key Things to Remember:

- There's no one-size-fits-all approach to parental involvement. Each family may have different constraints and priorities, but the key is to find ways to actively engage parents in their children's education. Parents should be active even if their schedule is busy with other responsibilities.
    1. One thing you can do is volunteer and work on different projects as they relate to your child's school.
- Attend at least 3 or 4 monthly PTA meetings each school year.
- Keep in touch with your child's teachers, especially in Middle and High School; these two stages are really important.
- Attend school board meetings regularly. The PTA can have a parent attend a meeting to represent the PTA board.
- There is No Wrong Way to PTA.
- All Children - One Voice!

Use these acronyms while facilitating and pondering your next move.

4-P's
- Partnership
- Persistent
- Powerful
- Performance

4-C's
- Communication
- Connection
- Create
- Consistency

**6 Keys Areas of Concern for Parents
to stay PLUGGED into:**

1. **Formula for Parent Success**: Remember this formula as you plan your schedules: Monthly PTA +1 ½ hours rather Zoom or in person = less than 12 hours per school year.
2. **Cyberbullying and Social Media demands**: Parents must navigate the challenges of cyberbullying and monitor their children's online activities. It's essential to create a positive digital environment and promote responsible social media use. Parents and schools will always be confronted with the difficulties of cyberbullying and the social media demands in the constantly changing world of technology. The internet may be a breeding ground

for negative thoughts and harmful comparisons,
so parents must remain proactive in managing and
monitoring their children's online activities.

3. **Academic Achievement Stress**: The stress
levels of parents' and children have increased due
to the growing focus on academic success. Parents
frequently find themselves in a difficult situation
where they must support their child's academic
progress while also making sure that their mental
health is taken care of. It becomes increasingly
difficult for parents to keep a positive attitude about
school in the competitive academic environment.

4. **Mental Health Awareness and Stigma**: Addressing
mental health issues among students requires breaking
down stigma and silence, while promoting open
dialogue even in the face of misunderstandings and
opposition from the community. Parents play a vital
role in advocating for their children's mental health
needs. Parents and students are facing increased
stress related to balancing academic success.

5. **Balancing Extracurricular Activities**:
Finding a balance between extracurricular
involvement and maintaining a healthy lifestyle is
essential to prevent burnout among students.

6. **Access to Quality Education**: Parents, particularly
in underserved communities, must advocate for
equitable access to resources, trained educators,
supportive learning environments, and opportunities in
education. Fighting against educational inequalities is
a collective effort that requires ongoing advocacy and
collaboration. In a society where educational inequalities

endure, parents can find common ground in the fight
to guarantee equitable opportunity for all children.

By addressing these challenges and working together as a
community, parents can play a significant role in supporting their
children's academic success and overall well-being. Remember,
every child deserves a voice and an opportunity to thrive in their
educational journey.

Chapter Seven: Final Thoughts

The Struggle for Parents

Who would have thought that in a world dominated by technology, where playgrounds are now virtual, our children would need cell phones just so we can feel secure while they're away? The struggle is real. Our educational system has become a battleground for dedicated educators fighting for our children's futures. Did you ever imagine it would be like this?

I started this handbook to help parents understand what's truly important in this new landscape. The COVID-19 pandemic has dramatically changed the educational foundation, revealing both strengths and weaknesses. Twenty-five years ago, I began my journey as the first Community Outreach Coordinator in my community's middle school district, excited about the possibilities. I approached the job with a blank canvas, fully aware that parents' involvement is the ultimate gift to our children and our educational system.

Parents have the power to change their children's schools if they aren't serving their children's best interests. Title 1, a policy from the Department of Education, has been around for decades to ensure parents understand that their input is essential. The struggle for parental involvement often stems from parents' day-to-day obligations. I understand this struggle because I've lived it. Emotional preparation for daily responsibilities is crucial for parents to be available for school events or PTA meetings. Some districts accommodate parents' schedules, recognizing the importance of their involvement in their children's education.

Single parents, in particular, must navigate numerous challenges, making school meetings a lower priority. In this world of teacher shortages, educational issues, and school shootings, the struggle is real. These challenges have become significant issues, and the only way to address them is for parents to take a stand, advocate for better policies, and support their children's education. Parents should feel comfortable sending their children to school without fear. Working with your local PTA, State PTA, National PTA, and government at all levels is essential for making meaningful changes.

The Balancing Act Parents as Providers

The most important job for parents is ensuring their children's education and being their primary providers. In this world of insanity, balancing raising a child and providing a safe environment for them to grow has become a delicate act. Parents are their children's first educators, laying the groundwork for various life paths. This is what parents strive to accomplish every day.

Parents are their children's first and foremost advocates, providers, defenders, and educators. Children learn and are nurtured by their parents, who may include biological parents, adoptive parents, guardians, grandparents, aunts, uncles, or caregivers. Regardless of the specific role, if you love and care for a child, you are their life's ultimate gift. This gives you the unique opportunity to witness and guide your child's development into a remarkable individual.

You might wonder how this handbook can help you understand the importance of becoming a warrior for your child and other children in your community. Parenting today has evolved significantly compared to decades ago. Today, we have many opportunities for ourselves and our children. Unlike previous generations, we don't have to endure the same extended processes our parents and grandparents faced. Yes, today's world presents unique challenges and complexities, but it also offers new possibilities.

It's essential to recognize the need to invest time and effort into making positive changes for our children. Despite the struggles and challenges, parents hold significant power when it comes to their children's education. By dedicating time and energy to understanding and addressing the issues around us, we can create a better future for our children.

Keeping It Real

As parents, navigating today's world has become more challenging. Technology makes many things easier, but keeping our children safe has become harder. Growing up, life felt simpler despite the lack of instant access to information and resources. Keeping it real is something I strive to accomplish as a parent educator, ensuring parents maximize every opportunity available to them and their children.

Parents often find it difficult to stay involved due to various challenges and inconveniences. However, opportunities always exist to support all children. During my time in education as a Parent Coordinator, I constantly thought of ways to spark parents' interest in being hands-on, particularly at the 9th-12th grade levels.

Supporting our children is crucial as it helps them understand the importance of receiving a quality education. If parents rotate their schedules to attend PTA meetings via Zoom or in person, we can collectively support students struggling in multiple areas. This support can provide educators with the assistance they need to ensure classrooms are adequately equipped to help all families. It may also offer a safety net for our teachers and students.

Engaging with new technology is beneficial and necessary, but it can also be a distraction. This reflects my old-school vs. new-school thoughts: we want our children to be safe and receive a healthy, well-deserved education. Politics has complicated the educational system, creating obstacles that obscure our goals. I witnessed the transition years ago when new teachers felt ready to become educational leaders after just one or two years in the classroom. While aspiring to leadership is commendable, it's important to balance new-generation teaching methods with the wisdom and experience of veteran educators. A solid foundation is essential; otherwise, everything will crumble.

Keeping it real means allowing ourselves to grow and understanding that we don't have to tear everything down to implement new methods. Ensuring our children receive a great educational experience while staying safe and secure is paramount. This involves giving credit to the individuals who make this possible: parents, administrators, teachers, and, most importantly, our children.

Providing A Safety Net for Children with Special Needs

I am genuinely passionate about this part of the handbook: parents being strong advocates and providers for their children. Early detection of special needs in a child's development can significantly benefit their long-term outcomes. Parents play a crucial role in ensuring their children have access to every available resource. When children with special needs are correctly diagnosed, creating an Individual Education Plan (IEP) can genuinely help them navigate all challenges.

An Individual Education Plan (IEP) is a program developed to ensure that a child with an identified disability attending an elementary or secondary educational institution receives specialized and related services. This definition is vital because the IEP is often seen as a compiled assessment based on evaluations conducted by professionals in various fields. It serves as a blueprint provided to the school and the child study team to ensure the necessary support is in place, helping the child succeed at every stage of their progress.

According to the Department of Education guidelines, the IEP should improve teaching, learning, and results when done correctly. Each child's IEP describes the educational program designed to meet their unique needs. This section looks closely at how the IEP is written, by whom, and what information it must contain at a minimum. You can find more detailed information about this process on the Department of Education's website: Department of Education IEP Guide.

The specifics outlined in the IEP can provide our children with the necessary tools to succeed. It's crucial to ensure that allocated funding is used effectively to support our children in every learning area. Parents should dedicate at least 16 to 20 hours a year to their child's school by attending PTA meetings, IEP meetings, and other curriculum meetings geared toward helping their child. As I mentioned earlier, parents are the most crucial part of the IEP Team besides their children.

If you have children, being their strongest advocate will require you to devise a plan that works for the family. Ensure you have access to your child's IEP at your fingertips as a guide to help you understand what is happening and why. Schools are educational institutions that provide our children with the most significant opportunities to succeed in every area of their lives, and parents play a vital role in making this happen.

This section of the handbook is dedicated to helping parents of children with disabilities understand the importance of their child's IEP program. Having the IEP document readily available on your laptops or phones for easy access is essential. The IEP structure helps in many ways, but if the document is not used effectively, you will see no changes in your child's educational development. This access allows you to ask questions or schedule a Zoom or in-person meeting. Always look for additional tools developed and researched by other professionals to help your child.

Most schools have PTA or Parent Group meetings designed to help you have more intimate discussions with other parents and professionals in this area. You can gain valuable insights from other parents who may be in similar situations.

I want to share my personal experience in this area. I have a beautiful granddaughter who has been diagnosed with autism. She is the first in our family to have a diagnosis that requires our attention and support to help her navigate these stages. When my family found out about this, I spent nights researching what others were sharing about this particular diagnosis. I quickly realized that many families experience autism on different levels. Having an educational background helped me understand the language in my research. I learned that there are many kinds of autism, and the more I am exposed to what is happening in this area, the better I can support my granddaughter

The National PTA.org website has fantastic resources and information to help you learn more about families experiencing the challenges that sometimes come with helping our children. As you continue to use this handbook as one of your guides, the practices outlined in this book apply to everyone who reads it. The goal is to help each parent, guardian, and caregiver be the Greatest Influence as it relates to being an Advocate for your children.

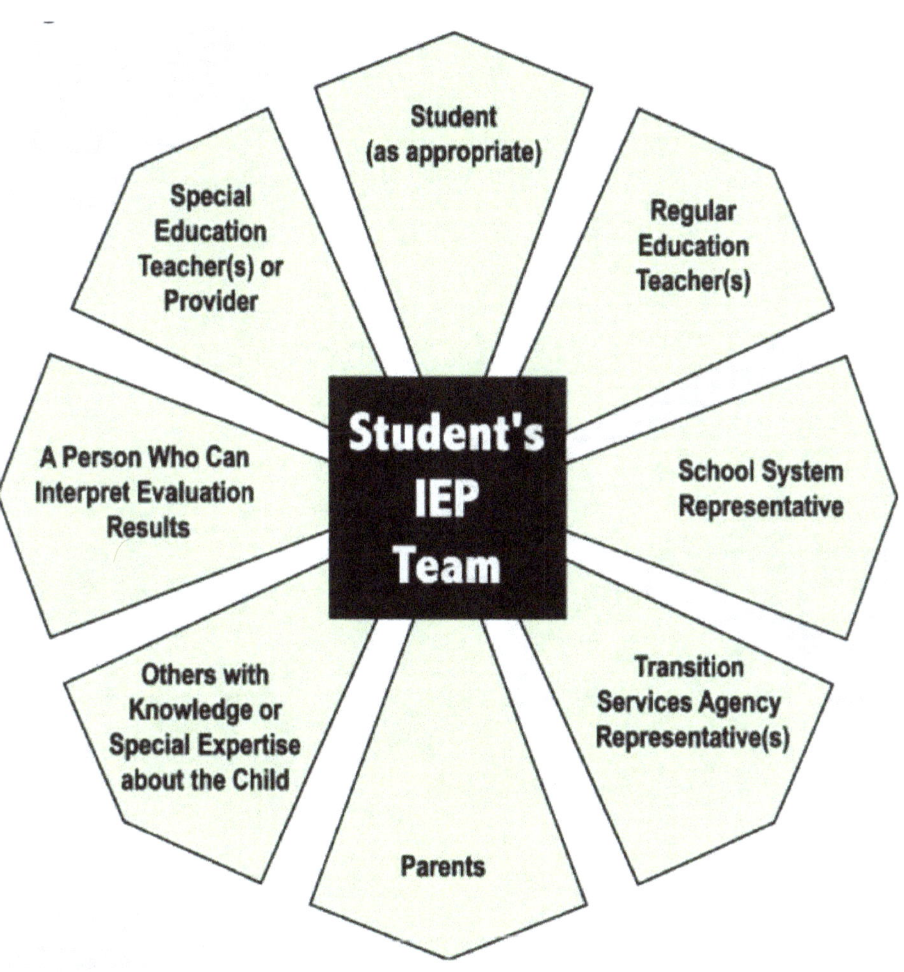

This picture shows a representation of the student's IEP team.

Notes

About the Author

Delores A. Wallace has been a passionate advocate for parents, students, and teachers for over 30 years. Her journey began in East Orange, New Jersey, where she worked as a Teacher's Assistant in Special Education. Over the years, she held various roles in education, including the first Community Outreach Coordinator for the East Orange School District.

Ms. Wallace holds a bachelor's degree in psychology from the University of Phoenix and an MBA from Strayer University. Her educational background, combined with her extensive experience in the field, has equipped her with the knowledge and skills to effectively support families and enhance parental involvement in education.

Throughout her career, Ms. Wallace has demonstrated a remarkable ability to bring people together. She has worked tirelessly to bridge the gap between parents, teachers, and the community, believing that collaboration is key to student success. Her efforts have resulted in the establishment of strong parent-teacher associations and partnerships with local businesses and organizations.

One of Ms. Wallace's notable achievements was the creation of a community event that celebrated children while providing valuable resources and support. The event, which included a fashion show aimed at boosting students' self-esteem, became a beloved tradition in the East Orange community.

In addition to her work within the school district, Ms. Wallace has been actively involved in county-level organizations such as the Essex County Youth Services Commission and the Workforce Development Council. She has served as a liaison between these organizations and the parents in her district, ensuring that families have access to important resources and information.

Ms. Wallace's philosophy centers around the belief that every parent is a gift, and every child is a blessing. Her dedication to empowering parents and supporting students reflects her commitment to building a brighter future for all.

Testaments

Dr. Tennellie Raney

"Ms. Wallace is a result-driven executor. Over the years, I have watched her move mountains for children under extreme circumstances. If you partner with her, she will get the job done."

Towanda Edwards, Realtor
Professional-Community Leader

"I have had the distinct pleasure of knowing Delores for many years. Her genuine, loving, and caring spirit attracted me to her. She is personable, reliable, and a true servant leader. She consciously brings like-minded individuals together, builds relationships, and increases your resources and networks! She is the PLUG!"

Kienast White-Parent (PTA Treasure 2004-2021, Fashion Show-Financial Manager)

"There are so many things to say about Ms. Wallace. I had the pleasure of meeting this remarkable woman at Newark Tech Vocational High School in 2004/2005 when my daughter and son attended. At that time, Ms. Wallace was a Parent coordinator, and I joined the PTA and later became PTA Treasurer under her leadership. I have also assisted Ms. Wallace with her Annual Fashion Show at the school, where she later started her own production company called Plug Entertainment LLC . Ms. Wallace is a beautiful lady with great spirit. Ms. Wallace has a way of drawing people into whatever she has going on at the time, and they never leave her side. She inspires you to reach

beyond every measure."

Nicole Walters-Parent

"Ms. Wallace's love for children is so strong. Every child in her path makes them see a side of themselves that they never knew they had. She helps the students know their dreams can come true if they genuinely believe in themselves. That is what makes her so unforgettable."

Miarah Beverly -Personal Note

"Miss Delores is among the most impressive and professional parent education consultants I have ever encouraged. She is not only knowledgeable and hardworking, but she is also more personable and more accessible to work with. She prioritizes her learner's interests and treats their needs as hers. In this context, Miss Delores is a highly responsible, reasonable, and reliable educational personnel. Due to current changes in education systems, most parents, especially the aged, need help understanding current forms of education; Miss Delores, compassionately and with much care, guides every person based on their understanding. This makes her the best parent education consultant one could encounter. In addition to being compassionate and caring, she employs various instructional strategies based on every learner's needs. This kind of enthusiasm and knowledge makes her indispensable in her sessions.

Nonetheless, on performance, Miss Delores is the best. She fosters positive relationships among the learners. She also exhibits initiative, authenticity, and creativity, reflecting the learners' community. This ensures the creation of a suitable learning environment for all students. Last, Miss Delores ensures that all her students receive equal opportunities to succeed. If you are a parent there and need an education consultant, Miss

Delores is your solution."

Ephraim Renee-Alumni Student

"Mrs. Wallace is the rarest gem. She has significantly changed and impacted my life for the better. Her endless wisdom and invaluable counsel have ignited a fire of progression that keeps me pressing forward. She has helped mold me into a champion. I am so thankful for her."

Sidney Barnes 111- Business Owner

"In many creations of our energy forces, we try to find souls that can provide comfort to our minds, and we can deliver information for growth. Ms. Wallace has done this in thousands of ways for many who need her presence and knowledge. Ms. Wallace has delivered excellence with no effort of recognition, and many who have graced her presence have been better because of it. Her professional life has reflected this unconditionally numerous times."